This workbook supports recovery from many addictions.

First, it is a straightforward guide to recovery from alchoholism.

It is especially helpful for typical difficulties on the fourth step. This is a thorough, clear and concise moral inventory when completed.

Other problems have special sections of their own in the book:

- gambling
- food-related
- anger and relapse
- problems with 'people, places and things' for recovery programs

By the time I met Pat Peterson, I had been in and out of recovery a number of times and at each juncture I was exposed to a 12-step process that was implemented with slight variations. I thought I'd seen it all. When I started working the steps using Pat's method, it was more intense. The raw emotions and insightful honesty brought about a personal transformation that has blessed me with the ability to stay clean and sober for eleven plus years now. Once I quit using, Pat's process allowed me to address my other glaring character defects in a timely manner, and I spend more time trying to give something back to others instead of seeing what I can get out of them.

Peace,

Tall Tom

Ellis Unit, Huntsville, Texas

12 Step Workbook

M. V. "Pat" Peterson

Emerald Ink Publishing
Hot Springs, Arkansas

Copyright © 2006, 2014 M. V. Peterson

Quantity and special purchase inquiries should be addressed to:

Emerald Ink Publishing, P O Box 2161, Hot Springs, AR 71914
501-538-7459
E-mail: emerald@emeraldink.com.

Neither House of One Foundation nor the publishers of this workbook take credit for the creation of the material that is found in this book. The author has told us that the material originated with other workbooks, seminars, and personal realizations that occurred while sitting in the groups. Any one who has studied workbooks about doing the Twelve Steps will recognize the similarity to words used in other workbooks. This material was created through an evolutionary process—the identification of individual references has been long lost. We cannot give individual credit but thank all those who have given of their time and creative skills to help those of us who are in the process of learning about ourselves and recovering from our obsessive-compulsive nature.

The Twelve Steps are reprinted and adapted with permission of Alcoholics Anonymous World Services, Inc. (A.A.W.S.) Permission to reprint and adapt the Twelve Steps does not mean that A.A.W.S. has reviewed or approved the contents of this publication, or that A.A.W.S. necessarily agrees with the views expressed herein. A.A. is a program of recovery from alcoholism _only_ — use of the Twelve Steps in connection with programs and activities which are patterned after A.A., but which address other problems, or in any other non-A.A. context, does not imply otherwise.

Edited by Linda Lee

Library of Congress
Cataloging of Publication Division
101 Independence Ave, S.E.
Washington, D. C. 20540-4320

Library of Congress Cataloging-in-Publication Data

Peterson, Milton V., 1944-
  A 12 step workbook / by Milton V. Peterson.
    p. cm.
  ISBN 10: 1-885373-58-9
  ISBN 13: 978-1-885373-58-8
  1. Behavior modification--Handbooks, manuals, etc. I. Title: Twelve step workbook. II. Title.
  BF637.B4P58 2005
  616.86'03--dc22

                    2005004635

Printed in the United States of America

Dedication

*Dedicated to incarcerated men and women
around the world.*

You are not forgotten.

The Twelve Steps
of
Alcoholics Anonymous

1. We admitted we were powerless over alcohol—that our lives had become unmanageable.

2. Came to believe that a Power greater than ourselves could restore us to sanity.

3. Made a decision to turn our will and our lives over to the care of God as we understood Him.

4. Made a searching and fearless moral inventory of ourselves.

5. Admitted to God, to ourselves, and to another human being the exact nature of our wrongs.

6. Were entirely ready to have God remove all these defects of character.

7. Humbly asked Him to remove our shortcomings.

8. Made a list of all persons we had harmed, and became willing to make amends to them all.

9. Made direct amends to such people wherever possible, except when to do so would injure them or others.

10. Continued to take personal inventory and when we were wrong promptly admitted it.

11. Sought through prayer and meditation to improve our conscious contact with God as we understood Him, praying only for knowledge of His will for us and the power to carry that out.

12. Having had a spiritual awakening as the result of these Steps, we tried to carry this message to alcoholics, and to practice these principles in all our affairs.

Contents

Preface

You will become aware, as you read through this material, that the words alcohol, drugs, and mood-altering chemicals are used randomly.

When I began my stay as a substance abuse counselor on the Ellis unit, I realized the institution was not going to allow me to segregate all the different "-isms" that I was to treat. Although I have a background of the twelve steps and traditions of Alcoholics Anonymous, it became evident very quickly that I was not going to be able to segregate my inmate clients. I also realized that finding a convict who had an addiction to just one chemical would limit my capacity to serve. With this realization, I began editing the steps to support recovery from many addictions. I focused on treating the illness of obsessive/compulsive disorder, which had resulted in chemical dependence and addiction in many of my incarcerated patients.

As I was working and living the steps myself, knowing that—as part of my disease—I often feel separate from everyone else, I realized that keeping someone out of my groups because of narrow parameters would only support and increase that person's belief that they were different and separate. That isolation (separateness) is a key component for moving into a relapse mode. I wanted the men to see what they had in common with each other, not what was different among them.

I understand and respect all of the twelve step programs now available to the public. I do not wish to dishonor their positions with this text and respect the parameters they have to enforce to keep their integrity.

Thanks for understanding,

Pat Peterson

The Process

In March of 1990, Pat Peterson, a licensed chemical dependence counselor and a recovering addict/alcoholic, was hired by the Texas Department of Correction to work on the Ellis Unit as a Substance Abuse Counselor. At that time, the Ellis Unit was the home of death row for the state of Texas. The unit also housed about two thousand more inmates in the general population. Sentences served at Ellis are usually very long.

Pat brought with him a few open-ended questions relating to the Twelve Steps of Alcoholics Anonymous and a belief to receive the benefits of these steps, one must work them and not just study them. With this belief, he started a group called a "Step-do-group," open to all prisoners. The men were encouraged to take the actions that recovering folks know often results in a right way of thinking! The only requirement for entering the group was a desire to do the steps. With this simple beginning, a miracle began to evolve.

As the men began doing the steps and receiving positive results from their actions, word got out about the program. People began asking to become a part of the group; before long, another group formed. As time passed and the groups became an integral part of the substance abuse program, another phenomenon occurred. Most Texas prisons are not air-conditioned; as the summer temperature rose in East Texas, so did the interest in the program. Because the classroom assigned to Pat's new recovery groups was air-conditioned, men began wanting in the group to get a little cool. Many men joined the group for this reason, but the rule was: they had to do the steps if they wished to remain in the group. They soon began getting the results of doing the steps. As the men began to get more comfortable with exposing themselves to their peers, they started feeling better about themselves, and with that, hope was born within them. Surprisingly, when the weather cooled off, they stayed in the group.

This process on the Ellis Unit lasted eight and a half years with as many as sixty men being in these groups at any given time. Usually one step would be given per meeting, by one inmate. The only requirement of the other members was to honor the bravery of the member doing the step by giving him their attention.

Many times a member would work the first three steps and then quit the group (citing other things they needed to be doing). In a few months, they would return, asking to be admitted back into a Step-do group. Pat would admit them, asking where they would want to begin. In most cases, they'd say step one. Many of the men tried this path of working the first three steps, stopping only to return and do them again. These men were laughingly called the "Texas Three Steppers. With the encouragement of their peers, many of these men moved on to the fourth step, then completed the others.

Throughout the years, Pat personally practiced the principles of the steps and realized that he was evolving, too. In his quest to help others, he became the recipient of experiences he had only dreamed of. He was able to confront all those parts of himself he had earlier refused to accept. As he began to love and accept all the character defects of the men, he started the process of loving and accepting all those same aspects of himself.

Hundreds of men passed through Pat's group. Where the seed of recovery was planted, it could not be removed, needing only attention to be activated. No one who completed even one of those steps will see themselves in the same manner. In every day life, whether it is on a prison unit or in the free world, a part of them knows if they ever decide to change, a tool is available in the way of the twelve step program.

Just as the book *Alcoholics Anonymous* and the A.A. twelve steps were the result of the effort of the first one hundred members, this workbook is the result of the effort of incarcerated men.

Step 1

*We admitted that we were powerless over alcohol—
that our lives had become unmanageable.*

There was a very good reason that the founders of the AA program placed the emphasis on powerlessness over alcohol. Many times we have observed people taking powerlessness for granted or with a casual attitude. Understanding powerlessness must be the foundation for any successful approach to the recovery from chemical dependency.

We cannot deny that there can be—and often is—a psychological as well as a physical dependency upon alcohol and other mood-altering chemicals. The medical profession verifies psychological dependency, and it is important to note the stress aspect of the addiction. To be specific, as dependent people we have an "urge" to use our chemicals of choice. We all probably started using chemicals for many of the same reasons: to relax, to have fun, to be part of a group, to be accepted. Not one of us started using any type of chemicals with the express purpose of becoming addicted.

Reluctance to examine our powerlessness is as much a symptom of the addiction as liver damage, withdrawal, digestive disorders and incarceration. We often tell ourselves and others, "But I don't need to drink: I don't drink all the time." Social pressures centered on the myth that "willpower" is all that is needed to control a drinking or drug problem can result in unwillingness to study our powerlessness.

An honest look at these symptoms will help us understand powerlessness. It will also help us deal with the self-deceiving shadow of fear that surrounds our chemical use.

Understanding and accepting powerlessness is a way to freedom. We will be releasing ourselves from the insanity, the morning shakes, the loss of respect and the loss of interest in activities that have been important in our lives. Dependent people have an x-factor. This is physical powerlessness. No one knows exactly what the x-factor is or why it exists.

As we develop a thorough understanding of alcoholism and chemical dependency, we will begin to understand our personal powerlessness over that disease. The reward of doing each one of the twelve steps is the return of a principle, which may be long forgotten. The principle gained in Step One of any twelve-step endeavor is Honesty.

POWERLESSNESS

How has the use of mood-altering chemicals endangered your life or the lives of others? List three separate instances.

1. _____
2. _____
3. _____

Names three behaviors that you are ashamed of as a result of your alcohol/drug use.

1. _____
2. _____
3. _____

What is it about your behavior that your spouse, family, and friends objectto most?

1. _____
2. _____
3. _____

Give some examples of how you have tried to control your use of mood-altering chemicals.

1. _____

2. _____

3. _____

Give some examples of how you have lost control of your behavior as a result of using mood-altering drugs.

1. _____ .

2. _____

3. _____

List some times when you started out "in control" but then "lost control" by drinking or drugging more than you intended and suffered the consequences.

1. _____

2. _____

3. _____

Can you recall any episodes when you were not taking mood-altering chemicals and those around you were? What did this feel like?

1. _____

2. _____

3. _____

Has there been any physical abuse to yourself or to others as a result of your use of alcohol/drugs?

1. _____

2. _____

3. _____

Why would you want to stop using alcohol/drugs? If so, give three reasons.

1. _____

2. _____

3. _____

Name three things you have blamed for your problems instead of your drinking/drugging.

1. _____

2. _____

3. _____

Name three ways in which you have attempted dealing with life's problems by avoiding your alcohol/drug problem.

1. _____

2. _____

3. _____

Name three ways in which you have delayed a real commitment to your alcohol/drug problem.

1. _____

2. _____

3. _____

UNMANAGEABILITY

What does "unmanageability" mean to you?

_____

How has your life become unmanageable in the following areas?
How do you see yourself?

_____

How have you managed your relationship with your family?

_____

How have you managed your relationship with your friends?

_____

How have you managed keeping jobs for long periods of time?

_____

How have you managed your physical health?

_____

How have you managed your spiritual life?

_____

How have you managed your sexual life?

_____

If you continue to use mood-altering chemicals, what do you think will happen?

1. _____

2. _____

3. _____

What goals have you set for you life?

1. _____

2. _____

3. _____

Do you feel that these goals are achievable if you continue to use mood-altering drugs?

_____

List three feelings that you have tried to alter through the use of mood-altering chemicals.

1. _____

2. _____

3. _____

Step 2

Came to believe that a Power greater than ourselves could restore us to sanity.

Coming to believe in a power greater than ourselves restores hope. In the past, we have hoped for positive results by placing our faith and trust in our own abilities to run our lives, and that has proven worthless. Our hope was often misplaced in people who we should never even say hello to. We hoped drugs and alcohol would make our lives better and even felt better for a time, but mood-altering chemicals have never done everything for us that we thought they would. If we are to recover from the disease of addictions, we need to actively place our faith in a power greater than ourselves.

At first, it may seem unrealistic to place our faith in a power we cannot see or touch, but that power is easily seen when we honestly look for it. Often, the first example of higher power working in our lives is the recovering alcoholic/addict standing right beside us! Sponsors and mentors provide a powerful example of sobriety in action. We accept our personal powerlessness over drugs and alcohol by allowing the group to guide us into the first returns of sanity. We soon discover that recovering folks are willing to help us do together what we have never been able to do alone, get clean and sober.

Step Two often delivers our first real spiritual experience on the road to recovery.

We gain the principle of the *hope* that we too can change for the better.

Describe your understanding of your Higher Power.

_____

Explain what a spiritual experience is to you. How do you think it differs from an emotional or physical experience?

_____

Describe a spiritual experience you have had. What did it feel like?

_____

In the past, in who or in what did you believe would make your life better? Give examples of the lengths you went to seeking this out.

_____

Looking back, do you now believe these goals were accomplished?

_____

What sequence of events led you to stop having Faith or Trust in yourself, others or things around you and begin to seek out a spiritual way of life?

_____

How do you expect your Higher Power to treat you?

_____

What does the word faith mean to you? How do you know you have faith?

_____

Give an example when you acted in faith. What did it feel like?

_____

How can faith help you accept and trust in a power greater than yourself?

_____

List recent events or a situation that indicate your faith is being strengthened.

_____

What does Sanity mean to you? How would you like to be different?

_____

Have you ever blamed God for anything that happened in your life? If so, what do you think about that situation now? Do you have resentment toward God?

_____

What makes you think you can't manage your own affairs?

_____

How does your relationship with God improve your competence in dealing with your life?

_____

If you had an interview with God, what would you ask? What would you want to know about your standing with God? What would you tell God?

_____

Step 3

Made a decision to turn our will and our lives over to the care of God as we understood him.

The Third Step is a turning point where we decide to give up our self-will and seek the care of a Higher Power much greater than ourselves.

It is time to acknowledge our need for a God's presence in our lives. We make the *decision* to surrender our thoughts, (our will), and actions, (our lives), over to the care of a God of our own understanding. He/she becomes our new manager, and we begin to accept life on his/her terms. He/she offers us a way to live that is free from the emotional pollution of our past, thereby allowing us to enjoy new and wonderful experiences. Step Three provides us with an opportunity to turn away from behavior that fosters addiction, discouragement, sickness and fear.

The gift of doing Step Three is the principle of *faith*!

The serenity prayer shows us exactly how God will help us when we make the decisions to seek his care. It is an expression of faith.

> *"God, grant me the serenity*
> *to accept the thing I cannot change,*
> *the courage to change the things I can,*
> *and the wisdom to know the difference."*

As we do Step Three, our faith increases and fear subsides, because our decision to make a commitment to Step Three brings a bit of calm into our everyday lives. We begin to see some of the things about us that need to be changed. We begin to feel the faith that God can show us how to make those very personal changes.

List any fear you have about doing the Third Step. If you are not aware of any fears, think again about the words "turn our will and our lives over..."

Do you have a history of being a trusting person as related to doing what you are asked to do?

_____

What does surrender mean to you? What feelings do you have about the word?

_____

How does it feel when you do what someone else wants you to do?

_____

Do you have a history of doing what others want?

_____

What problems do you think you will experience when you start doing someone else's will?

_____

Give three examples of behaviors you have given up in the past three months. If you can't think of any examples state behaviors you would like to give up.

1. _____

2. _____

3. _____

What will you lose if you turn you "will" and "life" over to the care of God? What will be the rewards or benefits?

_____

What is the feeling you are experiencing when you are not in your will?

_____

Which parts of your life are you most willing to turn over to God?

_____

List some recent examples when you turned your will over to your Higher Power and acted in faith.

_____

How are you going to know when your "will" has been turned over to the care of your Higher Power?

_____

When you get an idea that there is something you need to be doing, how do you know if your Higher Power is talking to you or if it is your ego speaking to you?

_____

What do you expect to happen as a result of taking this step?

_____

What is your definition of being "strong-willed"?

_____

Who are the people in your life that have control over your will power, and why?

_____

Do you seek to control others? If so, who are they, and what fears are driving you to control them.

_____

Are you able to express yourself honestly and openly when you need to? If not, why?

_____

Are you able to sense when you are receiving guidance to act upon?

_____

Do you trust guidance that has no "proof" of the outcome attached to it?

_____

What fears do you have associated with Divine guidance?

_____

Do you pray for assistance with your personal plans, or are you able to say, "I will do what heaven directs me to do"?

_____

What makes you lose control of your own will power?

_____

Write a Letter

Write a letter to your Higher Power. Include in that letter at least the following:

> What you are thankful for.
> What you are sorry for.
> What you are angry about with your Higher Power.
> What you need from your Higher Power.
> What you want from your Higher Power.

Step Three Prayer

Dear God, I turn my life over to you,
To mold me and do with me as you will.
Trusting that you will guide my steps.
I enter the world with help
That I may better do your will.
I welcome your holy spirit's power, love and guidance
    in everything I do.

Amen

Step 4

Made a searching and fearless moral inventory of ourselves.

Part A

Step Four (like each of the steps) marks the beginning of a new way of life. It says that today I will begin to take a realistic assessment of myself. Let this guide help you begin to learn to know yourself.

The *principle* gained in Step Four is *courage*!

Three attitudes are important: to be searching, fearless, and moral.

- Are you searching? Are you digging into your own self-awareness and describing your behavior as it really is?

- Are your fearless? It takes courage to face yourself in terms of what has truly been going on in your life.

- Do you know right from wrong? Take a good look at the "good-bad" implications of your behavior. How does it size up with your own values?

Take a searching and fearless moral inventory, but try not to be judgmental of yourself. You have already started to accept the good and bad aspects of yourself. You have experienced both sides of human behavior. Give yourself permission to accept these traits and to continue on your path of recovery.

You have chosen—in order to recover and better know and understand yourself—to take a walk through your life. Please don't limit yourself to simply answering the question, but rather tell the story of your life.

INSTRUCTIONS

A bit of advice on how to write: the hardest way to write a Fourth Step is with the Fifth in mind. Write your inventory certain that no one will ever read it. That is the only way to be fully honest. As soon as you think of sharing this writing with someone, you will color what you write, making yourself look like what you would rather be than who you really are.

For your convenience, the Fourth Step has been divided into three parts. Work on Part A, and when you have completed it, contact your sponsor.

Use abbreviations when it helps you jog your memory about a story. If you feel it is necessary to write out the whole event, use all the additional paper you need.

May your Higher Power be with you and strengthen you during this walk through your life.

HONESTY

What does being honest mean to you? Explain.

Are you honest with yourself? Explain.

Do you consider yourself an honest person? Explain.

Do you consider most people to be honest? Explain.

Is it all right to be dishonest sometimes? Explain.

Is it safe to be honest all the time? Explain.

Are you dishonest sometimes? Explain.

Were your parents ever dishonest to you? Explain.

Were you ever dishonest with your parent, wife, children, relatives, friends?

How do you treat a dishonest person? Explain.

Do you have friends that are honest or dishonest? Explain.

Do you consider your wife/spouse to be basically honest? Your parents/children? Close friends? Explain.

Can *not* saying anything be a dishonest act? Explain in what instances.

Today, is it in your best interest to be as honest as you can be? Explain.

RESPONSIBILITY

What does responsibility mean to you? Explain.

Who did you consider to be responsible when you were growing up? Explain.

Who were you responsible for when you were growing up? Explain.

What were your responsibilities at home while growing up? At school, at church, with your friends, neighbors? Explain.

Did you like your responsibilities as a child? Explain.

As a teenager, how did these responsibilities change? Explain.

As a teenager, did money have anything to do with responsibility? Explain.

Did you like your responsibilities as a teenager? Explain.

As an adult how did these responsibilities change? At home? At work? marriage/ children/ community/ friends/ relatives? Explain.

Has your attitude changed toward responsibility as an adult? Explain.

Do you consider yourself a responsible adult? if yes, in what areas? If no, in what areas? Explain.

Are you responsible to yourself? Explain.

What areas do you think need improving? Explain.

Do you value responsibility? Explain.

What are those values? Explain.

If you think/feel responsible for someone, how do you treat them? Explain.

Do you treat people differently who you feel responsible for? Explain.

Have you ever felt solely responsible for a solution /answer to a problem? Explain.

MONEY

Have you ever wished you had more money? Explain.

Have you ever envied people who have more money than you? Explain.

Have you ever had any problems concerning money? (bill, debts, etc.)

Are you uncomfortable when you are short of money? Explain.

Did your mother teach you anything about money? Explain.

Did your father teach you anything about money? Explain.

Was money a problem in your family while growing up? Explain.

Did your parents control you with money? Explain.

Have you ever stolen money from your parent/guardians? Explain.

How important was money in your family? Explain.

Have you ever performed sex for money? Explain.

Have you ever hurt anyone over money? Explain.

Have you ever been hurt by anyone over money? Explain.

Did you ever perform any illegal act thinking you were going to receive money? Explain.

Is money a part of being responsible? Who taught you? Explain.

Presently, to what lengths are you willing to go to get money? Explain.

Did you ever lie to get money? To keep from giving up money? Explain.

Are you comfortable with your present behavior concerning money? Explain.

List your good points concerning money.

PROCRASTINATION

What does procrastination mean to you? Explain.

Have you ever put off until tomorrow something that you needed to do today?

Were your parents procrastinators? Explain.

Did you see your parents start and finish jobs/tasks? Explain in what areas (for example: cleaning house, washing clothes, mowing yard, home when they said they would be, doing what they said when they said it would be done).

Today, do you have a habit of completing things you start? Explain.

Today, do you think you are incomplete? Explain.

Today, do you wait till the last minute to do things? Explain.

Today, are you working on your procrastination? Explain.

JUDGMENT

What does being judged mean to you? Explain.

Have you ever been judged by others? If so, explain.

How do you judge others in the following area? (race, sex, gender, economic, religion, home town, clothes)

Have you ever formed an opinion about someone or something because of something you learned or heard through the media or some other source? Explain.

Step 4

Made a searching and fearless moral inventory of ourselves.

Part B

Step Four (like each of the Steps) marks the beginning of a new way of life. It says that today I will begin to take a realistic assessment of my self. Let this guide help you begin to learn to know yourself.

Three attitudes are important: to be searching, fearless, and moral.

- Are you searching? Are you truly digging into your own self-awareness and describing your behavior as it really is?

- Are your fearless? It takes courage to face yourself in terms of what has really been going on in your life.

- Do you know right from wrong? Take a good look at the "good-bad" implications of your behavior. How does your present behaviour compare with your values?

- Take a searching, fearless, and moral inventory but try not to judge yourself. You have already started to accept the good and bad aspects of yourself. You have experienced both sides of human behavior. Give yourself permission to accept these traits and to continue on your path of recovery.

You have chosen to take a walk through your life in order to recover and better know and understand yourself. Please don't limit yourself to simply answering the question, but rather tell the story of your life.

INSTRUCTIONS

A bit of advice on how to write: the hardest way to write a Fourth Step is with the Fifth in mind. Write your inventory certain that no one will ever read it. That is the only way to be fully honest. As soon as you think of sharing this writing with someone, you will color what you write, making yourself look like what you would rather be than who you really are.

After you have given this B part of Step Four to your sponsor, you will be ready for the C part of this step.

Use abbreviations when it helps you jog your memory about a story. If you feel it is necessary to write out the whole event, use all the additional paper you need.

May your Higher Power be with you and strengthen you during this walk through your life.

LOVE

What does love mean to you? Explain.

How do you express love? Explain.,

Where did you learn your present concept of love? Explain.

How do you treat the people you say you love? Explain.

Who do you love? Explain.

Have you ever been loved? Explain.

Do you love yourself? Explain.

What "things" have you ever loved? (cars, drugs, clothes, food, etc.)

Can you love someone you can't totally accept? Explain.

Would you like someone to continue to love you despite the fact that some of the things you do are not acceptable to him or her? Explain.

FEAR EXERCISE

Fear is a underlying cause of many forms of spiritual disease. Wide ranges of mental and physical ills are frequently the direct results of this unwholesome condition. Learning to acknowledge fear in a healthy way is an important part of our recovery process.

List situations in which fear is a problem for you. Answer the following questions when describing these conditions:

What or whom do you fear (people, institutions, place, things)?
Why are you fearful (what happened to cause this fear)?
How has this fear affected you (lowered self-esteem, difficulty in relationships, diminished goals, procrastination)?
Which character defect is active (approval seeking, control, fear of abandonment)?

Use this form to list all of your fears.

I fear _____

because _____

this affects _____

This activates _____

I fear _____

because _____

this affects _____

This activates _____

I fear _____

because _____

this affects _____

This activates _____

I fear _____

because _____

this affects _____

This activates _____

I fear _____

because _____

this affects _____

This activates _____

I fear _____

because _____

this affects _____

This activates _____

I fear _____

because _____

this affects _____

This activates _____

I fear _____

because _____

this affects _____

This activates _____

RESENTMENT

Resent means to "Re-Feel." Resentment is an emotion (anger, frustration, fear, shame, guilt, embarrassment, dislike) that you experience and hold onto. You will have that feeling again when you are reminded of that incident. It is like watching a video tape over and over. We feel the same pain each time we recall the person, place or experience.

Have you ever been wronged or disrespected by someone? Explain.
When you see them, do they remind you of what happened to you? Explain.
What feelings do you experienceg at that moment? Explain.

Resentment is an underlying cause of many forms of disease. Our mental and physical ills are frequently the direct result of this unhealthy condition. Learning to deal with resentment in a healthy way is an important part of our recovery process.

List situations in which resentments are a problem for you. Answer the following questions when describing these conditions:

What or whom do you resent (people, institutions, place, things)?
Why are you resentful (what happened to cause this resentment)?
How has this resentment affected you (lowered self-esteem, loss of employment, difficulty in relationships physical harm or threats)?

Use this form to list all of your resentments.

I resent _____

because _____

this affects _____

This activates _____

I resent _____

because _____

this affects _____

This activates _____

II resent _____

because _____

this affects _____

This activates _____

I resent _____

because _____

this affects _____

This activates _____

I resent _____

because _____

this affects _____

This activates _____

VIOLENCE

What is violence to you? Explain.

Can there be verbal violence? Explain.

Were you spanked or whipped as a child? Was this sexually embarrassing?

What does sexual violence mean to you? Explain.

Were you ever spanked or whipped while naked? Explain.

What instrument was used in your punishment as a child? Explain.

As an adult, did you ever have to discipline a child? If so, explain. (What type of instrument did you use?)

How many times have you threatened a child with bodily harm for discipline purposes? Explain.

When you were young, did you ever have money taken from you? Explain.

Have you ever forced yourself on someone for sex? Explain.

Have you ever had sex after being told no? Explain.

Have you ever hit, bitten, or scratched your partner while having sex? Explain.

Have you ever been bitten, hit, or scratched by your partner while having sex?

Did you ever use the threat of violence to obtain sex? Explain.

Were you ever spanked by a adult when you were young? Explain.

As an adult have you ever had money or property taken from you? Explain.

Did you ever threaten someone to get money? Explain.

Did a schoolteacher, coach, principle or nun ever physically discipline you? Explain.

Have you ever been physically harmed by law enforcement? Explain.

Have you ever been physically harmed by adult neighbors, friends of parents or other relatives? Explain.

As a young person, did you ever physically attack or show an act of violence (throw rocks, etc.) toward another person, institution, school police station, physical buildings? Explain.

Where did you learn to use violence to control others? This can be physical or verbal violence. Explain.

Do you still use the same methods now? If so, explain.

What is the difference between acts of violence and implied violence? Explain.

Have you ever stalked anyone? Explain.

Have you ever used "being responsible" as a reason to be violent with someone (attacking your significant other or children because you feel responsible to teach them)? Explain.

How many people have you taught a lesson by using physical or verbal violence against them? Explain.

As a young person did you ever act out of violence in front of your peers for approval? Explain.

Have you ever acted violently (physically or verbally) toward someone because of his or her religion, race, sexual preference, gender, money, hometown? Explain.

Have you ever acted out violently because you were angry? Explain.

AUTHORITY FIGURES

Fear of people in roles of authority can be a result of our parents' unrealistic expectations of us—wanting us to be more than we were able to be. We see people in authority as having unrealistic expectations of us and fear we cannot meet their expectations. We are unable to deal with people whom we perceive as being in positions of power. We often misinterpret simple assertiveness displayed by others as anger. This can cause us to feel intimidated and to become oversensitive. No matter how competent we are, we compare ourselves to others and conclude that we are inadequate. As a result, we constantly compromise our integrity in order to avoid confrontation or criticism.

Who was the boss when you were a child? Explain.

Name the people who had power/control over you when you were growing up (parents, brothers/sisters, relatives, teachers). Be specific by names. Could be more than one.

What did you learn from each of these experiences? Be specific.

Do you still see these people a authority figures? Which ones and explain.

Presently who do you think has power/control over part of your life? be specific and explain.

Do you act the same when talking with your boss or someone you look up to as when you are with your peers? Explain why not?

How do you act when in the presence of an authority figure? Be specific and explain.

Have you ever been aggressive to someone in authority? Be specific and tell the story.

Have you ever been in the presence of an authority figure and feel confidant, secure and feeling/thinking you are getting a fair deal? Be specific and explain.

Are you able to accept guidance from authority figures? Explain.

ABANDONMENT

What does abandonment mean to you? Explain.

Do you think you have ever been abandoned by your mother, father, friends, grandparents, society, husband/wife? Explain.

Have you ever done something illegal for someone because you were afraid they were not going to accept you? Explain.

What does emotional abandonment mean to you? Explain.

Is it possible to be emotionally abandoned (when you are sad, no one is there for you)?

Do you feel you have ever been emotionally abandoned? Explain.

How many people have emotionally abandoned you? Explain.

Have you ever been in a room full of close friends or relatives and felt alone or as if you were by yourself? Explain.

CONTROL

As a child, did you ever have a tempter tantrum? Explain.

As a child, did you ever act sick to avoid school, church, visiting relatives? Explain each. What were you trying to control? Explain.

When you were being disruptive in school, what was the payoff or what were you trying to control? Explain.

What did you do to gain others approval (play sports, join gangs, join youth groups? Explain.

If you were in organizations, were you always one of the leaders so that you could keep control? Explain.

Does being in control make you feel safe? How is it working?

How do you feel when you're not able to control others? What is going on around you? Explain.

Do you dislike change? What does control have to do with this? Explain.

How would you feel about changing jobs? A geographical change?

Have you ever tried to control your family or spouse by making them feel guilty or ashamed? Explain.

In what ways can you control people verbally? Explain.

Have you ever played the victim with family and friends to control your money situation? Explain.

Have you ever told someone to stop crying? Explain.

Do you need to control your physical surrounding? Explain.

Do things need to be your way to be happy? Explain.

PRIDE

What does pride mean to you? Explain.

What does self-pride mean to you? Explain.

What does false pride meant to you? Explain.

Has pride been your enemy in the past? Explain.

Has pride ever stopped you from apologizing? Explain.

How has pride stopped you from seeing/hearing the truth? Explain.

How many times has your pride hurt others? Explain.

How does pride interfere with your honesty? Explain.

How many times have you refused to take a job because it was beneath you?

How many times have you refused to take advice because you were afraid you would look stupid? Explain.

Does pride keep you from seeing others as equals (race, gender, sex, economic, home town, educations)? Explain in each instance.

Does pride keep you from getting medical attention? Explain.

How did pride keep you from seeking recovery earlier? Be specific.

How has pride limited your spiritual experiences? Explain.

How many times has self-pride kept you from asking for help (family, friends, spouse)? Explain.

Are you proud of your accomplishments in school? Have you ever cheated on a test? Explain.

Can you be proud and humble at the same time? Explain.

Can you be proud and avoid issues you think are important? Explain.

Can you care about someone and still be proud? Explain.

Do you pride yourself on being a "good person"? Explain.

Step 4

Made a searching and fearless moral inventory of ourselves.

Part C

Step Four (like each of the Steps) marks the beginning of a new way of life. It says today I will begin to take a realistic assessment of myself. Let this guide help you begin to learn to know yourself.

Three attitudes are important: to be searching, fearless, and moral.

- Are you searching? Are you truly digging into your own self-awareness and describing your behavior as it actually is?
- Are your fearless? It takes courage to face yourself in terms of what has really been going on in your life.
- Do you know right from wrong? Take good look at the "good-bad" implications of your behavior. How does it size up with your own values?

Take a searching, fearless and moral inventory, but try not to be judgmental of yourself. You have already started to accept the good and bad aspects of yourself. You have experienced both sides of human behavior. Give yourself permission to except these traits and to continue on your path of recovery.

You have chosen in order to recover and better know and understand yourself, to take a walk through your life. Please don't limit yourself to simply answering the question, but rather tell the story of your life.

INSTRUCTIONS

A bit of advice on how to write: the hardest way to write a Fourth Step is with the Fifth in mind. Write your inventory certain that no one will ever read it. That is the only way to be fully honest. As soon as you think of sharing this writing with someone, you will color what you write, making yourself look like what you would rather be than who you really are.

Use abbreviations when it helps you jog your memory about a story. If you feel it is necessary to write out the whole event use all the additional paper you need.

May your Higher Power be with you and strengthen you during this walk through your life.

RELATIONSHIPS

Your Family

Take your mother's inventory, listing all the things that are wrong with her. All the things that you would like to change to improve her. Now list all the things you liked about her.

List all the things throughout your entire life (but especially in childhood) that your mother did to hurt you. List all the things for which she should make amends to you. Do not justify her actions—if they hurt you with or without a good reason on her part, list them.

List all the actions on your part that hurt your mother—all through your life. This should include all the things for which you will have to make amends to her. Again, do not justify. If you felt then or now that the actions were wrong, list them.

Take your fathers inventory, as you did with your mother.

List all the things your father did to hurt you.

List all the things you did to hurt your father.

If either parent is dead, write out your memories of walking through the illness, death and funeral. Tell how you heard of the illness and death, how you felt at the funeral, how you feel now about your parent being dead.

If your parents are divorced, or separated, with which one did you live? How did you feel about being with this parent? Did you play your parents against each other to get your way? Did you feel responsible to bring them back together? Did the parent with which you were raised want you? How did and how do you feel about all this today?

If you had stepparents or foster parents, take the inventory of each of them. Did they resent raising you because you were not their child? If they had their own children, did they treat you differently? How did you feel about being in their home? How do you feel about them today? List all that they owe amends to you for. List all that you owe amends to them for.

If you were not raised by your parents for any considerable length of time, where you remember it or know about it from others write about the experience—and how you feel about your parents not raising you during this period.

If you spent some time in an orphanage or children's home, take the inventory of the supervisors of the home and the adults directly in charge of you. Again, list any hurt they did to you and the reason for any amends you owe them.

Now take the inventory of every one of your brothers and sisters, living and dead. Start with the oldest and work to the youngest. Cover your entire life. for each of them, tell what you don't like about their personality, briefly tell what they have done wrong with their lives. Tell if you like them now and tell about any wrongs you ever did to them.

Now take inventory of their spouses. Be brief, but be sure to include any arguments you ever had with them, any sexual advances, any injuries.

Take inventory of all your stepbrothers and sisters including half brothers and sisters.

Take the inventory of each of your grandparents. Tell how you saw them as a child. If you feared or disliked going to their home. If you were raised by any of them for an important portion of your life, go into greater detail on any unpleasant memories you have of this period. Also, talk about the good memories you have of this period.

Take inventory of your mother's family, describing briefly any problems you have had with them.

Take inventory of your father's family, describing briefly any problems you have had with them.

Is your family close today? Do you exchange presents? Calls? Do you get together? How do you feel about this? Do you miss closer family ties? Do you feel your family interferes too much in your business?

Are you proud of your family blood? Are you proud or ashamed of your racial makeup? Do you blame your parents for what you're not proud of—for making you Polish, Catholic, Black, or something else?

Were you ashamed to bring friends into your home? Why? Were you ashamed of the way either of your parents looked, spoke, dressed, acted? Did your parents or guardians encourage you to develop your talents? Did they discourage you by putting you down or surrounding you with fears? Are they proud of your success? Do they belittle it? Do they pressure you to succeed to overcome their feelings of failure? Are they proud of you?

FRIENDS

Take inventory of your friends (past & present), talking about how they treated you and if you have any anger or resentment at any of them.

What motivates you to go into a relationship with someone (sex, money, security, home, children, information, loneliness)?

How many long-term relationships do you have? Explain.

How many people do you call "my friend"?

How many friends have you abandoned in fear of being alone (you left someone before they left you)?

SEX

CHILDHOOD SEXUAL HISTORY

What, if any, memories do you have about sex and sexuality from birth to age 5? From 6 to 10? From 11 to 18?

Were both of your parents happy that you were born a boy/girl?

Were you happy being a boy/girl as a child? Why/Why not?

Were you ever punished or shamed for childhood sexual play?

Was bedwetting or soiling ever a problem for you?

How old were you when you started into puberty? Was adolescence awkward? Did you get appropriate and reliable sex education?

Did anyone make fun of your sexual development—too fast, too slow?

Was anyone invasive about your sexual development—took too much interest in your breast/penis were too big or too small?

When did you start bathing yourself? After that did you have privacy in the bathroom?

Did you ever think someone might be spying on you when you were bathing or getting dressed?

Did you ever spy on anyone bathing or getting dressed?

Who was the first person of the opposite sex you saw naked?

Would you say someone sexually abused you during childhood? Who? What did he/she do? Did you tell? What happened when you told?

What was your most sexually embarrassing moment during childhood?

What was your first experience with pornography?

Were you ever photographed naked or in seductive poses?

Men: Were you ever dressed up like a girl?

Women: Were you ever dressed up like a boy?

Did you ever see or hear your parent having sex?

How much did you know about your parent's sex life?

Women: did you ever have an accident with your menstrual period?

How old were you when you learned the facts of life? How did you get this information? How did you find our about masturbation?

When was the first time you stimulated yourself sexually?

When did you masturbate for the first time? When did you have your first orgasm?

Men: Did you know about "wet dreams" before you had one? Did anyone ever threaten to harm your penis?

Did anyone make sexual innuendoes or tell inappropriate sexual jokes around you?

What was adolescence like with respect to dating and romantic and/or sexual experiences?

What was your first post-puberty sexual experience? Were drugs or alcohol a part of that experience?

Were you spanked or whipped as a child? Was this sexually embarrassing or sexually invasive?

ADULT SEXUAL HISTORY

What are your attitudes and views about sex? Where did you get them? Are you comfortable discussing sex? Was your family comfortable talking about sex?

Are you comfortable with your body and sexual attractiveness?

Do you generally feel guilty about your sexual thoughts, feelings, or behaviors?

Do you feel guilty about a specific sexual behavior? What behavior?

Do you have a problem saying "no" to sex when you don't want it?

Can you talk to your partner about your sexual needs and wants?

Have you ever been concerned or confused about your sexual orientation—straight or gay?

Have you ever been concerned or confused about your sexual identity? Male or female?

What role, if any, did alcohol or drugs play in your sexual experiences during adolescence or your adulthood?

What is the role of alcohol or drugs currently playing in your sexual encounters?

How do you see yourself sexually: Oversexed? Undersexed? Uptight? Frigid? Compulsive/out-of-control? Guilt ridden? Scared? Ugly? Uninterested? Impulsive? Powerful? Really good at it?

Do you have one sexual relationship after another?

Have you ever had a sexual affair? Is this a problem for you?

Has your partner had sexual affairs?

Do you or have you ever had several sexual relationships going on at the same time?

Do you do "one-night stands? Do you engage in anonymous sex?

Do you engage in phone sex?

Do you like to watch others having sex?

What do you think of group sex?

Do you enjoy anal sex?

Have you ever used a pet or animal in a sexual experience?

What kind of sex toys, if any, do you use for sexual pleasure?

Describe your ultimate romantic /sexually fulfilling experience?

Do you fantasize during sex or during masturbations? What sexual fantasies are the most exciting?

What is the most exciting part of a sexual experience?

What, if any, are your sexual "hang ups"?

RELIGION

What do you think of organized religion?Do you dislime any church or churches particularly? Explain.

As a child, what church did your parents belong to? What do you feel about that church now?

Did any priest or minister hurt you in any way? How? List each and every clergyman you resent with the reason or reasons you resent them. Do the same for any other church official, Sunday school teacher, youth leader, choir master.

Describe the picture of God, which you received as a child. Would you want to be this type of person?

According to the teaching given you as a child, list some of the things for which God sends people to hell. Would you send your mother or your daughter to hell to suffer forever for doing those things? What does this tell you about your God?

How often were you sent to church as a child? How did you feel while there? Did you start skipping church services? Did you stop going? Did you get caught? What happened?

How do you feel about the efforts of other churches to influence your life?

Were you married in a church? Yours? How did you feel about the clergyman? The ceremony?

Did a clergyman bury your parents? Was the service adequate?

What churches did you join on your own? Do you hold any resentment about these churches? Why?

Are you attending a church now? Do you feel guilty if you're not? Do you feel comfortable if you are? Is the God of your church as good as the God of the program?

If you believe in the God, do you become angry when people attack God, church, or clergymen? Do you try to argue people into believing in God?

If you don't believe in God, do you become angry when those who do believe talk about their beliefs? Do you feel superior to those who believe?

If you don't attend church, are you hurting your children by making it more difficult for them to be introduced to God?

Have you blamed God for all the pain that brought you to the program?
Have you forgiven God for all this pain? Is there some tragedy for which you still can't forgive God? Are you willing?

Did nuns ever teach you? Do they scare you? Are there any you still resent?
Did any church official ever make sexual advances toward you? How do you feel about this today?

Have you ever hated God? Cursed him? Why?

Have you ever been sure he would damn you?

How do you feel about Him now?

Tell what you believe about your God today.

Step 5

*Admitted to God, to ourselves, and to another human being
the exact nature of our wrongs.*

This step requires a dramatic "leap of faith" for most of us. The thought of sharing our innermost secrets with our higher power is scary enough, and telling another person exactly what we have done to get ourselves into our present predicament is downright threatening!

We calm ourselves with the knowledge that millions of others have done this step and moved on up to a life of recovery from the disease that cripples us.

Our newly made decision to seek God's guidance in Step 3 leads us to review our written fourth step work with our Higher Power (HP) at our side. We begin to see the common threads in our debilitating behavior that often started in childhood. These commonalities uncover the "exact nature" of our character defects for us. The "other human being" involved in this step often shows us what corrections need to be made.

Here is an example: A fellow wrote in his fourth step that he was in prison because he was a drug addict, that if he wasn't hooked, he wouldn't have been arrested, therefore the drugs were to blame. Upon review with his higher power and his other human being in Step Five, he came to a new understanding of his criminal behavior. He later said that he now understood that the exact nature of the wrong that put him in prison was not his drug addiction but his extreme need for power. He acknowledged that he sold drugs because he loved the super-heated feeling of demanding that "junkies" grovel before him begging for a "fix." He admitted that he often required the trembling addicts to participate in unspeakable sexual acts or terrible crimes in order to deserve his services. He got off to being God in the lives of very sick people.

The personal reward for completion of Step Five is the principle of *integrity*. We've put our honesty into action.

Have I reviewed my Fourth Step work in the quiet of my own mind? Do I have any new revelations to add to my personal inventory?

_____

_____

_____

Exactly where and when have I decided to review my written moral inventory with the God of my own understanding?

_____

_____

_____

Who have I asked to hear my Fifth Step?

_____

_____

_____

Why do I trust this "other human being" to guide me through Step 5?

_____

_____

_____

What do I expect to gain from this examination of my wrongs?

_____

_____

_____

Step 6

Were entirely ready to have God remove all these defects of character.

To be successful with Step Six, we must sincerely desire to change our disabling behavior. Our past has been dominated by our self-will, rarely calling on God or anyone else for help. By recognizing our life condition and being honestly determined to eliminate our behavior flaws, we see that self-will has never been enough to help us. In this step we become ready to accept help and relinquish our self-destructive nature. We acknowledge that it is time to grow up!

If we have been searching in our moral inventory, we now should have a list of character defects, which have been causing our destructive behavior and emotional problems. We also know that some of these shortcomings are not of our own making, they were pounded into us from childhood. Now is the time to decide if we are willing to surrender these defects of character to gain peace of mind and serenity. It would seem obvious that we would be willing to give these up, but old habits die hard.

Willingness is the principle we seek in this step, and it is the reward.

Explain your commitment to changing your behavior. What are you willing to do to change?

_____

_____

_____

Give examples of how each of your character defects has caused problems for you or those around you. Be specific.

_____

_____

_____

Which character defect is causing you the most pain right now?

_____

_____

_____

How willing are you to give up this defect?

_____

_____

_____

What would you gain and what would you lose be giving it up? Be specific.

_____

_____

_____

Explain your commitment to changing your behavior. What are you willing to do to change?

_____

_____

_____

How willing are you to give up this defect?

_____

_____

_____

What positive attitude would you replace it with?

_____

_____

_____

What do you feel when you think of surrendering to God and trusting that he/she will remove your defects?

_____

_____

_____

Cite examples that indicate you are committing your way to the care and guidance of your Higher Power.

_____

_____

_____

In which areas do you have to work the hardest to give up your defects?

_____

_____

_____

What anxieties do you feel when considering having your character defects removed?

_____

_____

_____

Identify any character defects you are not entirely ready to have removed. Explain why you are attached to them.

_____

_____

_____

Why is it necessary to learn humility before God can remove your defects of character?

_____

_____

_____

List any doubts you have that are interfering with your readiness to have God remove your shortcomings.

_____

_____

_____

What do you fear will happen when your defects are removed?

_____

_____

_____

What behavioral changes have you made that indicate your thought patterns are changing?

_____

_____

_____

READINESS EXERCISE

The following exercise is intended to help you prepare to let go of the character defects you discovered when working Step Four:

Inordinate pride, conceit, disdainful behavior or treatment of others.

List examples that indicate you are willing to let go of your constant need to impress others.

_____

_____

_____

Greed, selfishness, excessive acquisitiveness, never having enough of anything.

_____

_____

_____

What do you fear you will lose by letting go of your intense desire for material things?

_____

_____

_____

_____

What will you gain by giving up your selfish tendencies?

_____

_____

_____

Dishonesty, deceit, disposition to defraud to deceive, justifying behaviors by explaining ourselves dishonestly:

How will honesty improve the quality of your life?

_____

_____

_____

What anxieties do you feel when you realize the need to tell the truth?

_____

_____

_____

Gluttony, covetousness: one given habitually to greedy or voracious acquisition of possessions; excessive eating or drinking

In what ways are you ready to lessen your desire for status and material wealth?

_____

_____

_____

What do you believe your life will be like when you no longer experience jealousy?

_____

_____

_____

Laziness: disinclined to activity or exertion; not energetic or vigorous; distinct avoidance of responsibility.

List examples that indicate you are willing to heighten your productivity.

_____

_____

_____

What steps have you taken to eliminate your habit of procrastination?

_____

_____

_____

Step 7

Humbly asked Him to remove our shortcomings.

The principle in Step Seven is "Humility". It is necessary to look at our past lives and see how we mismanaged our own will power. The mistakes we made in life often resulted in overwhelming humiliation by friends, family and society, so we tend to shy away from these old feelings and often confuse "humility" with humiliation. In reality there is nothing to fear in this step, when we are entirely ready to be changed.

To be truly humble, it is necessary to acknowledge a dependence on a Power greater than ourselves, and to be willing to ask for help. We accept the help as it comes to us day by day.

One recovering addict says to be prepared to be fully involved in the Seventh Step process when we humbly ask for the removal of a shortcoming. He thought HP would wave some magic wand or something and his *anger* would disappear. Instead, he was confronted with seven straight opportunities to be angry. A sponsor said, "Ask yourself just how much difference any particular upset will make in your personal life one year from now." When he was able to say those words to himself instead of retaliating, the heat went out of the incident and he kept his "cool." Today he has truly "ceased fighting everything and everybody" and is a happy man.

Many of us find that as a result of Step Seven, our defects of character fade and leave us over time. It is an evolutionary process.

What does the word "Humility" mean to you? Trust? Acceptance? Honesty? Looking for the good? Truth?

_____

_____

_____

Can you think of any humiliating experiences in your life that you now realize were learning experiences? Give examples plus the lessons you learned.

_____

_____

_____

List examples that indicate you are practicing humility.

_____

_____

_____

Have you tried giving up your defects using your will power? What were the results?

_____

_____

_____

What do you fear by not knowing what lies ahead?

_____

_____

_____

Make a list of the character defects, which you are willing to have removed by asking the help of your Higher Power.

_____

_____

_____

List areas in which you are discouraged about your level of progress in having your defects removed.

_____

_____

_____

What "things" were taken away from you as a child before you were ready to give them up?

_____

_____

_____

Describe your present relationship with your Higher Power.

_____

_____

_____

In what way does prayer relieve your feelings of anxiety?

_____

_____

_____

Cite examples that indicate you are focusing more on the God of your understanding and less on yourself.

_____

_____

_____

Which of your negative character traits are becoming positive? Explain how this change is making an impact on your life.

_____

_____

_____

What affirmations do you use as a part of your ongoing commitment to recovery?

_____

_____

_____

What changes in behavior have occurred as a result of working Step Seven?

_____

_____

_____

Write a letter to your Higher Power asking for the willingness to surrender these defects.

_____

_____

_____

Seventh Step Prayer

My creator, I am now willing
that you should have all of me,
good and bad.
I pray that you now remove from me
every single defect of character
which stands in the way of
my usefulness to you and my fellows.
Grant me the strength,
as I go out from here,
to do your bidding.

Amen.

Step 8

*Made a list of all persons we had harmed,
and became willing to make amends to them all.*

Making amends helps us let go of the past. If we are willing to make amends and do make them—we will be free to meet people and situations without fear. In this step, we review our Step Four inventory, our notes from Step Five and our list of known character defects from Step Six to prepare our list of those we have done wrong.

The ones we are closest to, our families and friends are usually those we hurt the most and they top our lists. Employers we cheated and stole from, companies and institutions we ripped off and the individual we maligned are also included. Any person or entity that causes us fear and pain when we think of them belong on our Eight Step list. We don't worry about how we'll make the amends at this point; we just want to honestly prepare a list of those who deserve our amends.

Love is a key ingredient in this step and our reward is the principle of Brotherly Love.

List what you believe the benefits will be to you in making these amends.

_____

_____

_____

Can you think of examples in your life when your unwillingness to make amends has caused problems? Give examples.

_____

_____ .

_____

What do you think making amends to yourself means? What will be the benefits?

_____

_____

_____

In what ways can you change your attitudes? To whom? Are you willing? Give examples.

_____

_____

_____

List situations in which you have cheated others. How will you make restitution?

_____

_____

_____

Cite examples of your passing judgment on others and harming them and yourself.

_____

_____

_____

Why does reconciliation with the God of your understanding require reconciliation with others?

_____

_____

_____

How does the God of your understanding fix you to love others?

_____

_____

_____

What do you expect to gain by giving to others?

_____

_____

_____

In what ways are you compassionate toward those who have caused you harm?

_____

_____

_____

What major character defects caused injury to yourself or others?

_____

_____

_____

What consequences do you fear in making your amends?

_____

_____

_____

Why is forgiving yourself an important factor in the amends making process?

_____

_____

_____

List the major ways in which you have harmed yourself.

_____

_____

_____

How will your recovery be hindered if you are unwilling to forgive yourself?

_____

_____

_____

Who/What I harmed _____

What I did _____

How I was wrong _____

My amends should be _____

Who/What I harmed _____

What I did _____

How I was wrong _____

My amends should be _____

Who/What I harmed _____

What I did _____

How I was wrong _____

My amends should be _____

Who/What I harmed _____

What I did _____

How I was wrong _____

My amends should be _____

Who/What I harmed _____

What I did _____

How I was wrong _____

My amends should be _____

Who/What I harmed _____

What I did _____

How I was wrong _____

My amends should be _____

Who/What I harmed _____

What I did _____

How I was wrong _____

My amends should be _____

Who/What I harmed _____

What I did _____

How I was wrong _____

My amends should be _____

Who/What I harmed _____

What I did _____

How I was wrong _____

My amends should be _____

Who/What I harmed _____

What I did _____

How I was wrong _____

My amends should be _____

Who/What I harmed _____

    What I did _____

    How I was wrong _____

    My amends should be _____

    Who/What I harmed _____

    What I did _____

    How I was wrong _____

    My amends should be _____

    Who/What I harmed _____

    What I did _____

    How I was wrong _____

    My amends should be _____

    Who/What I harmed _____

    What I did _____

    How I was wrong _____

    My amends should be _____

    Who/What I harmed _____

    What I did _____

    How I was wrong _____

My amends should be _____

Who/What I harmed _____

What I did _____

How I was wrong _____

My amends should be _____

Who/What I harmed _____

What I did _____

How I was wrong _____

My amends should be _____

Who/What I harmed _____

What I did _____

How I was wrong _____

My amends should be _____

Step 9

*Made direct amends to such people wherever possible,
except when to do so would injure them or others.*

Webster's dictionary says *amend* means to "change for the better." That's what we set out to do in this step. We take actions that not only change our part of damaged relationships, but we ourselves are changed for the better in the process.

"Real alcoholics" and addicts are among the most undisciplined people on the planet. Step Nine requires us to gather up the *principles* we gained in the previous steps and put them to work. We use all of the "honesty-open-mindedness & willingness," "patience, tolerance & understanding" we now have, to accomplish our amends. This is a very active process on our part and it is not accomplished overnight. Nor is a direct amend completed with a silly apology like: "Gee whiz-Gosh golly darn, I am so sorry" or "If you hadn't started the fight, I wouldn't have hit you." We've been making excuses like these all of our lives and no one in their right mind will ever believe such nonsense any more.

By the time we reach Step Nine, we are ready to contact those we have harmed. Our sponsor who has made his own amends is a great help. Our newly embraced higher power is always ready to show us the way. In fact, many recovering alcoholics say God will see to it that those folks we need to contact come into our view when we are indeed ready to make amends.

One "ex-offender" became an evangelist after prison. He'd been convicted of one armed-robbery and served his time for it, but he was also guilty of several other hold-ups in several states. As he traveled from town to town he often felt compelled to confess his crimes and he argued with his God, using his new wife and family as an excuse to keep his felonies a secret. Finally after several years of personal turmoil he walked into the office of every district attorney in every county where he'd gotten away with armed-robbery and confessed. He was released with good wishes by each and every court because the statues of limitations had run out or because the judge considered his time served and the quality of his life today, and was merciful. The slate was wiped clean. He remains a happy and successful man of God today.

The principle gained in Step Nine is *Discipline*!
What does making "direct amends" mean to you?

_____

_____

_____

Why is it so important that you make amends?

_____

_____

_____

How can giving back what you have taken be seen as making an amends?

_____

_____

_____

How has passing judgment on others caused them harm?

_____

What rewards to you expect to receive from making your amends?

_____

_____

_____

How do you distinguish between apologies and amends?

_____

_____

_____

List an example in which you apologized, but did not make amends.

Who on your amends list causes you the most anxiety? What is your concern?

_____

_____

_____

What is your reaction to the idea of making amends to your enemies?

_____

_____

_____

Describe how prayer or writing can help you to make amends where direct contact is not possible.

_____

_____

_____

Give examples of occasions when you offered hospitality to another without grumbling.

_____

_____

_____

Cite a situation in which direct amends could have serious consequences.

_____

_____

_____

How are you going to determine who to make amends to? How are you
going to determine if you harmed them?

_____

_____

_____

Cite instances in which being impatient to make an amends proved
harmful.'

_____

_____

_____

How will completing Step Nine enable you to bury the past and improve
your self-esteem?

_____

_____

_____

How do compassion, kindness, and patience contribute to the serenity in
your life?

_____

_____

_____

Step 10

*Continued to take personal inventory
and when we were wrong promptly admitted it.*

In Step Ten, we begin the maintenance segment of the steps. We sustain what we have accomplished, become more confident and proceed with joy along our spiritual journey. The first nine steps put our house in order and enabled us to change some of our destructive behavior patterns. By continuing our work on the steps, we will increase our capacity to develop new and healthier ways of taking care of ourselves and relating to others.

A review of our behavior is usually done at day's end. We enjoy the love we gave or received and acknowledged the good we did on this day. We thank God that we did not have a drink or use. We look for encounters that angered us, dark feelings that rose up, harsh words that were spoken and resentments that returned. We see that we are continuing to make progress while committing to correct any wrongs we made as soon as possible.

Since most negative encounters find that all parties were at fault in some measure, we vow to take responsibility for our words and actions with the folks involved. The more upset we are the more important it is to call our sponsor before we take remedial action. Our personal mentors often know exactly how to make a difficult situation right without rancor because they have been there. They've already made the mistakes as well as the progress we seek.

A sponsor related the new magic found in the "Wrong" in Step Ten; He says that when he told his twelve-year-old daughter that he was wrong when he embarrassed her in front of her girlfriends, she was astounded to hear her own father admit he was wrong, and they began a new relationship on that day. He found the courage to use the word wrong every time it was needed because of the acceptance he gained with his daughter. Troubled waters are calmed and admitting we were wrong often assuages feelings.

We gain the principle of *perseverance* in Step 10.

The program's emphasis on daily inventory is based on the realization that many of us haven't developed the necessary tools for self-appraisal. As we become familiar and comfortable with person inventories, we will be willing to invest the time required in exchange for the rewards received.

How will daily inventory help you develop the ability to appraise your behavior?

_____

_____

_____

How does taking a daily inventory support your spiritual growth?

_____

_____

_____

How does daily inventory improve your ability to get along with others?

_____

_____

_____

Can you think of examples from your life when a situation would have been eased if you had apologized immediately instead of letting the situation go on. Give three examples.

_____

_____

_____

Give three examples of when you have blamed others and not been willing to look at your part in the problem.

_____

_____

_____

Do you feel a strong need to be right? Explain.

_____

_____

_____

Give some examples of situations where replacing a character defect with a character asset would have been beneficial to your serenity.

_____

_____

_____

Make a list of the benefits you feel would be gained from doing a daily inventory.

_____

_____

_____

How much time do you spend alone reflecting on your life? How is it helpful in your recovery?

_____

_____

_____

What new defects have emerged as a result of your new experiences?

_____

_____

_____

How does daily inventory help you remain free of resentments and allowyou to deal with issues promptly?

_____

_____

_____

List examples where you have been misunderstood. Describe the feelings that resulted from maintaining your composure.

_____

_____

_____

What precautions are you taking to prevent becoming overly confident and falling into past behavior patterns?

_____

_____

_____

Have you been able to recognize and learn from the positive things you do each day? Give examples.

_____

_____

_____

Give examples of how your thinking has changed.

_____

_____

_____

Describe the changes you have made in your lifestyle.

_____

_____

_____

Describe how you interpret the world around you now as to how you were interpreting it five years ago.

_____

_____

_____

Step 11

Sought through prayer and meditation to improve our conscious contact with God as we understood Him, praying only for knowledge of his will for us and the power to carry that out.

Step Eleven is our opportunity to develop a deepening relationship with our Higher Power. Having developed this relationship in Steps Two and Three, we have been able to rely on our HP during the subsequent steps. The relationship we developed with our Higher Power is the source of courage and strength for doing the work suggested in all the steps.

Very few alcoholic/addicts have any kind of conscious contact with God as we begin our recovery. The very concept is foreign to most of us.

We often think of God as the great punisher who demands payment for all the wrongs we have committed. When we sit still and let our mind explore the possibility of a real higher power being active in our lives and even friendly towards us, we discover the power in this simple step. First, we see that HP doesn't want us to wallow in the sickness of alcohol and drugs. Then we see that we are just expected to be dues paying human beings capable of righting our own wrongs and helping others.

As we follow the Twelve Steps of Recovery we follow in the steps of many others who found a new life. We give up our old prayers of distress; "Please get me out of this mess and I'll be good forever" and learn to pray; "Thank you for my sobriety and my freedom, just show me what you want me to do today and I'll do it.

The Principle gained in Step Eleven is *God Consciousness*.

As a result of your diligence in working the Steps, what has been your experience in catching a glimpse of God's will?

_____

_____

_____

At this point in working the Twelve Steps, we have no doubt noticed that to "make a decision to turn our will and our lives over to the care of God" is not a single event. It is a daily routine. Now we are being asked to "pray for knowledge of His will for us and for the power to carry that out." Turning our will over may have been more of a challenge than seeking the knowledge of God's will for us. When infantile traits continue into adulthood, the person is referred to as being immature. The ego can be an obstacle for our emotional sobriety.

How have you experienced the realization that "knowledge of God's will" comes to you only as a result of your surrendering your will?

_____

_____

_____

If we are periodically puzzled by the daily challenges we face from "His Majesty the Baby," we must accept that we are adult children and are still growing up. The inner child tolerates frustration poorly, tends to want to do things in a hurry, and is impatient. The hallmark in our adult life is the tendency to be under pressure for accomplishments. Big schemes, and hopes abound. Unfortunately, these are not always matched by an ability to produce. We are clearly not doing God's will when we are expressing this behavior. "Like the cat with nine lives, the ego has a marvelous capacity to scramble back to safety, a little ruffled, perhaps, but soon operating with all its former self-confidence, convinced once more that now it, the ego, can master all events and push on ahead."

Identify behavior s that you continue to demonstrate as an example of "His Majesty the Baby."

_____

_____

_____

How does your ego get in the way of your relationship with God?

_____

_____

_____

Doing God's will may get so entangled with the reassertion of our old feelings and attitudes that our emotional sobriety becomes a shambles of discontent and restlessness. As we see this struggle in process, the need for our Higher Power becomes clearer.

What is your understanding of God's will for you at this point in your life?

_____

_____

_____

Step Eleven is where we focus on the daily process that is necessary for our spiritual awakening. We may have had spiritual experiences prior to this, but a spiritual experience is not a spiritual awakening. In fact, many spiritual experiences may be required before a spiritual awakening is possible. A spiritual awakening comes when we know there is a Higher Power that has been taking care of our wills and our lives and when we know we can depend on that Higher Power to run the show from now on.

What is your understanding of God's will for you at this point in your life?

_____

_____

_____

Identify situations in which you believe you have had a spiritual awakening.

_____

_____

_____

Step Eleven suggests that we improve our conscious contact with God, as we understand Him. In order to do this, we must have already established contact with him. We have made conscious contact with God at least three times in the earlier Steps. In Step Three, we admitted our wrongs directly to Him. In Step Seven, we humbly asked Him to remove our shortcomings. Step Eleven seeks to improve that contact, thereby enabling us to bring our Higher Power into our lives on a daily basis. It is now that we can begin to enjoy the quality relationship that is possible with Him.

How has your relationship with your Higher Power improved since you began working the Steps?

_____

_____

_____

In what areas do you have difficulty asking for guidance from you Higher Power?

_____

_____

_____

The program implies that our Higher Power is a loving power who has only the best interests of each individual in mind. The basic premise includes the idea that this loving power wants to enrich our lives. It is exciting to realize that we can have an abundant life if we accept the protection and care of our Higher Power. The A.A. pioneers believed that this abundant life could be had for the asking. "We found that God does not make too hard terms with those who seek Him." To us, the Realm of Spirit is broad, roomy, all-inclusive: never exclusive or forbidding to those who earnestly seek. It is open, we believe, to all.

Give examples that show your Higher Power to be a loving Power who has your best interests at heart.

_____

_____

_____

The means recommended to improve our conscious contact are prayer and meditation. These are the channels by which we reach Him and He reaches us. To pray is to petition God for what we would like Him to give us, and to ask for His guidance in our affairs. Prayer tells God what we want. Meditation is listening to God's will for us. Meditation techniques are designed to quiet our minds and rid us of our daily thoughts and concerns. In doing this, we allow God to enter into our minds so that we can hear His messages for us.

What are your past experiences of prayer when you petition God?

_____

_____

_____

What are your past experiences of meditation?

_____

_____

_____

Assuming we are willing, how do we pray, and what do we pray for? Many of us were taught to pray before we understood what it meant. In the beginning, we may have used the prayer "Now I lay me down to sleep, etc.". We asked God to bless Mommy and Daddy and significant others. As we grew up, some of our dreams shattered. We may have had a tendency to blame God for not answering our prayers. Based on the principles of the Program, our attitude toward prayer changes as we work the Steps. We learn to ask for God's will for us and to accept that He knows what is best. The old habit of praying for material things diminishes, and we replace it with prayers for guidance. We begin to rely on some of the slogans and prayers such as "Let Go and Let God" or the Serenity Prayer. Our prayers can be as simple as "God, please help me," or "Thank you, God." Any prayer is helpful if it helps the individual. The only requirement for a prayer to be successful is that it be sincere, humble, and not for our own selfish gain.

List examples of how you pray to God. How has your quality of prayer improved?

_____

_____

_____

In what ways do you feel uncomfortable when praying to God for help and guidance?

_____

_____

_____

Meditation is an ancient art that entails quieting the mind and not thinking. It is the channel through which we receive guidance from God. In order to meditate successfully, we must be willing to quiet our conscious mind and to remove the barriers of our conscious thoughts. This is difficult for some of us because we are unaccustomed to sitting still and relaxing energy we normally expend in keeping our emotions in high gear and our bodies rigid.

Because you have opened your mind to inspiration, in what ways have you discovered that meditation can reveal solutions you had not dream of?

_____

_____

_____

In what ways has Step Eleven changed your view of the method or use of prayer and meditation?

_____

_____

_____

The importance of Step Eleven is that it tells us precisely the things to pray for. In this Step of spiritual awakening, we pray only for knowledge of His will for us and for the power to carry that out. The word "only" emphasized the fact that from now on, we pray for nothing else except His will and the courage to go forward and do what He wants us to do.

What resistance do you experience when you read the part of Step Eleven, which states to pray "only" for knowledge of His will and for the power to carry that out?

_____

_____

_____

The miracle of this Step is that it changes our past method of praying into a form of meditation, whether we know how to meditate or not. Praying only for His will and for the power to carry that out drives all our personal concerns from our consciousness and allows us to concentrate only on His concerns. This very prayer empties our mind of our own wants and allows God to enter.

What thoughts have you had that you assumed were from God, only to discover that they were unconscious desires. (Praying for a new relationship leads us into past behavior)

_____

_____

_____

What was the result of acting on these illusions?

_____

_____

_____

If we have thoroughly placed our will in His care and pray, we must trust that our will is being directed by Him. The power to carry that out will be the courage to do so, and He will also give us that. Seeking guidance is a tricky matter because we are so accustomed to running our lives rigidly and making demands on God. Our own desires and opinions are so much a part of us that we are likely to view the will of a Higher Power in terms of our own feelings.

How is your own ego and self-will getting in the way of your praying for God's will?

_____

_____

_____

In Step Eleven, we concede complete willingness to accept God's will on whatever terms are offered. We are no longer in a position to demand anything, and the best we can hope for is relief from our agony. We stop making demands on our Higher Power and let things work out in a natural way.
Give examples that show you are not putting demands on your Higher Power and are willing to let things work out in a natural way.

_____

_____

_____

Prayer and meditation are used to improve our conscious contact with God, as we understand Him. If we are progressing satisfactorily with Step Eleven, there will be signs along the way. One sign is deep senses of gratitude, accompanied by a feeling of belonging in the world at last. Another is our feeling of being worthy. We have a sense of being guided and sustained as we proceed with our activities.

What is your opinion of your self-worth today?

_____

_____

_____

In what areas of your life do you have a sense of gratitude?

_____

_____

_____

It is not always easy to maintain this new way of life. We may face boredom and disillusionment after the early stages of inspiration and excitement. Step Eleven reminds us of the need to maintain the wonderful way of life we've been given. It is no quick fix. It is really Steps Two and Three practiced on a daily basis. It can be our guide for the rest of our lives. If we understand and follow it carefully, some of the changes in our lives will border on the miraculous. We can have continuous recovery along with the qualities we were seeking but never found.

How is boredom a problem for you now that you are achieving some peace and serenity in your life?

_____

_____

_____

Step Eleven does exact a price, and we must pay it if we expect favorable results. There is a price in giving up the self-will that led us into trouble. Part of the price is facing the need to become open-minded and being willing to change. Doing God's will can be as simple as accepting that there is no strain in doing God's will. As soon as we accept it as our own, we will experience complete peace and joy. Unless we experience this, we are refusing to acknowledge His will for us. And finally, Step Eleven calls for faith and persistence—the very qualities that we applied so wrongly to our compulsive behavior.

How willing are you to allow change now, compared to your willingness prior to working the Steps?

_____

_____

_____

What is your current level of faith and persistence?

_____

_____

_____

Give your thoughts and feelings now that you have finished this exercise.

_____

_____

_____

Step 12

*Having had a spiritual awakening as the result of these Steps,
we tried to carry this message to alcoholics,
and to practice these principles in all our affairs.*

The Twelfth Step is where we were headed when we started our journey toward recovery and a spiritual awakening. As we worked our way through the Steps, something inside told us that there was hope at the end of the journey. The mystery surrounding the Twelve Steps is that they really work for those who are willing *to surrender to a Higher Power. A.A. tells us: "The joy of living is the theme* of the Twelfth Step, and action is its key word." If we have practiced the other eleven steps to the best of our ability, we will have a spiritual awakening.

The principle we gain in Step Twelve is *Service.*

By the time we reach this step many other recovering addicts/alcoholics have been of service to us as we "trudge the road of happy destiny." Now we are truly ready and able to help others.

A recovering alcoholic in Houston, Texas relates that the fellow who "Twelve Stepped" him discovered the program while he was incarcerated in San Quentin prison in California. So when the Texan heard that it was possible to carry the message of recovery into Texas prisons he signed up saying that going inside the walls would give him the opportunity to give back the gift of recovery he received because an ex-convict helped him. He rounded up a sober "home boy" and they have now attended 12 step prison meetings together on a regular basis for twenty-five years. Both men agree that they get a lot more out of this "service work" than they bring into the prisons. They learn firsthand what is waiting for them if they ever return to booze and drugs.

Carrying the "message" to those who still suffer is the heart of personal recovery for millions of addicts/alcoholics today.

List three ways in which the Twelve Steps have helped you to experience the joy of living?

_____

_____

_____

The process of working the Steps can be likened to the transformation of a caterpillar to a butterfly. The caterpillar is not clear that it is going to be a butterfly. Everything that is part of its death and rebirth in the cocoon must be experience. The story is told of a man who noticed a cocoon on a bush in his yard. As he started to pull it from the bush and throw it away, he noticed the end was opening and a butterfly was struggling to escape. In an effort to help the emerging butterfly, he took it inside and carefully cut the cocoon away with a razor blade. The butterfly feebly crawled from the open cocoon and, with a few hours, died. It needed the strength it would have gained from the struggle to free itself in order to survive in the outside world. In a like manner, our working the Steps is something that only we can do. Any attempts to have another person do our work or find an answer for us inhibits our own recovery and limits our ability to become strong.

Explain your understanding of the butterfly story as it applies to your needs to have your own experiences.

_____

_____

_____

Our spiritual awakening is a gift that places us in a new state of consciousness and being. It is usually accompanied by a complete change in values. Where there used to be darkness, we now begin to see light. For most of us, the awakening is subtle and can only be viewed with hindsight. The maturity we gain by working the Steps enables us to view many experiences often painful as being spiritual in nature. Our awakening can be viewed as the sum total of these individual experiences. With each of them, we can identify in some way or another how our Higher Power is guiding us.

Which spiritual awakenings have been the most rewarding for you?

_____

_____

_____

How can you further enhance your spiritual awakenings?

_____

_____

_____

It is important to remember that our spiritual awakening is an ongoing process. It may have begun early in the Steps but it continues for the rest of our lives. It is not a distinct event with a clear beginning and ending. As our spiritual awakening continues, we become more lovable, make friends more easily, and feel more comfortable with people. Our relationships with our families improve as we draw close, yet we recognize each other's independent identity. We no longer have unrealistic expectations of ourselves, and we accept ourselves for who we are.

Evaluate your current relationships with your family and friends.

_____

_____

_____

How do these compare to your previous relationships?

_____

_____

_____

Because we know this program works and is working for us, we are ready to carry the message to others. This is the means by which the program grows, prospers, and flourishes. We have healthy tools for reaching out to these addicted people who are in bondage, as we once were. The message we carry is a liberating one. Sharing the message strengthens our own recovery and continues our spiritual growth.

Given that you have something to share with others, are you willing to carry this message to those in need? If so, how do you plan to do this?

_____

_____

_____

There is no formal qualification for working this Step, other than the willingness and the desire to tell our stories as honestly as we can. This is one time when being ourselves is the gift we give to others. This can happen anywhere when we are called upon to do volunteer work, share in meetings, or interact with coworkers and family members. As we share our story with others, it helps them to recognize their needs and we are learning to be humble and to express ourselves honestly. When we carry the message, we share how the Twelve Steps have transformed our lives, taking time to share our miraculous experiences with others who are in need of help. We tell them what we used to be like, what happened to us as a result of the Steps, and what we are like now. As we share our strength and hope with newcomers we help them find a way in solving their own problems, look at themselves honestly, and stop finding fault with others.

Given your expanded self awareness from working the Steps, how are you now clear that you will never have enough insight into another's life to tell them what is best for them *to do? Explain.*

_____

_____

_____

Working with newcomers can be a rewarding experience. These people are usually troubled, confused, and resentful. They are looking for "instant relief". They need guidance and we can help them to understand that the program represents pain and hard work. The rewards and miracles far outweigh the pain. We need to encourage the newcomers to be gentle with themselves and to take the program one day at a time. This is also a growth experience for us as we reflect back on where we were when someone introduced us to the program. When carrying the message, we must emphasized that the decision to join the program is an individual one that is made by most of us who have suffered enough, are tired of hurting, or in other words, have "hit bottom."

Are you clear that sharing with others can do more for you than it can for them? Explain how carrying the message is an obligation you have to yourself.

_____

_____

_____

A recurring message throughout the Twelve Steps us the importance of humility and obedience to our Higher Power. As we diligently practice these principles in our daily affairs, the key factor for success is our relationship with our Higher Power. Working closely with our Higher Power helps us stay on the right course by our considering Him as a sourced of guidance and support. We realized now that we cannot achieve peace in the world until we have achieved peace within ourselves. We cannot achieve peace and serenity within ourselves independently of a Higher Power. We must individually admit we are powerless and begin to work on our spiritual development one day at a time, for the rest of our lives.

Examine the degree to which you rely on your Higher Power. Give examples.

_____

_____

_____

We can view our progress by comparing where we were with were we are now. Are we less isolated and no longer afraid of authority figures? Have we stopped seeking approval and becoming accepting of ourselves as we really are? Are we more selective of the people we choose to form relationships with and are we able to keep our own identity while in a relationship? Have we developed the ability to express our feelings? Have our fears lessened? Have a lot of our character defects been transformed into assets, and are we behaving in a sane manner? If we are able to answer affirmatively to the above we have come a long way since Step One when our character defects were active and damaging.

Describe the progress you see in yourself as a result of completing the Twelve Steps.

_____

_____

_____

As we practice this new behavior in our daily affairs, life in general seems to start working better. For some of us, our examples in family and work environments have a positive effect on those around us and we can see recovery in our loved ones. This is truly a measure of our progress and of our determination to change our lives and our behavior. The more committed we are to living the Steps on a daily basis, the more likely we are to have a continual spiritual awakening for the remainder of our lives.

What changes do you see in your family and friends that you can attribute to changes in your own behavior?

_____

_____

_____

Relapse

As you spend more time in this program, you will notice that relapses are part of the growing process. It is very seldom that a person starts a learning process and does not fall short of expectation. So with this in mind, our problem may not be in falling short but how we react to that experience.

Nearly every person close to the addict is able to recognize behavior changes that indicate a return to the old ways of thinking. Often, individuals and fellow program members have tried to warn the subject, who by now may not be willing to be told. He or she may consider it nagging or a violation of his or her privacy. There are many danger signs. Most addicts, if approached properly, will be willing to go over an inventory of symptoms periodically with a friend of the program. If the symptoms are caught early enough and recognized, the addict will usually try to change his thinking, to get back on track again. A weekly inventory of symptoms might prevent some relapses. This added discipline is one, which many addicts seem willing to try.

Following are a few questions one must keep in mind while trying to go through this process called recovery. Remember, the only people who can't seem to work this program are those who cannot be honest with themselves. Good luck.

Name three instances before your relapse when you became tired (exhausted, maybe worked to hard, or the like).

_____

_____

_____

Give three examples of how you said some unnecessary little lies or deceits with your fellow workers or friends.

_____

_____

_____

Give three examples of some little lies you told yourself during this time.

_____

_____

_____

Give three examples of times when things were not happening fast enough for you or others were not doing what you thought they should be doing.

_____

_____

_____

Give three examples of you arguing small and ridiculous points of view. "Why don't you be reasonable, and agree with me?"

_____

_____

_____

Give three examples of when you became frustrated at someone because they weren't acting the way you thought they should.

_____

_____

_____

Give three examples of when you felt sorry for yourself.

_____

_____

_____

Name some times when you felt like you had it made. Ex. "I no longer have this problem" Be specific.

_____

_____

_____

Give some examples when you became complacent, when you gave up your disciplines because they were not necessary any longer.

_____

_____

_____

Give some examples when you were expecting too much of other people. Example: "I am changing, why aren't they?"

_____

_____

_____

Make a list of the disciplines you gave up in the last three months. Ex. going to meetings, talking to some one you trust, expressing your feelings, and so on.

_____

_____

_____

Give examples of some goals you set that were too high for you to reach. (Happiness is not having what you want, but wanting what you have.)

_____

_____

_____

Give three examples of how you have lost your gratitude.

_____

_____

_____

Explain how you have become omnipotent. That is when you have all the answers for yourself and others. No one can tell you anything. You ignore suggestions or advice from others. You hear preaching when someone is giving you other options.

_____

_____

_____

Anger

*We admitted that we were powerless over anger—
that our lives had become unmanageable.*

Give some examples of how you have tried to control other people through acting angry. List three separate instances.

_____

_____

_____

Give three examples of how you have manipulated people through your anger in order to control being in a particular place.

_____

_____

_____

Give some examples of how powerlessness (loss of control) has revealed itself in your experience while being angry.

_____

_____

_____

List some times when you started out happy and then became angry.

_____

_____

_____

Can you recall any episodes when you were not angry and those around you were? What did this feel like?

_____

_____

_____

Has there been any physical abuse to yourself or to others as a result of your anger.

_____

_____

_____

If you continue to be angry what do you think will happen?

_____

_____

_____

How has your anger endangered your life or the lives of others? List three separate instances.

_____

_____

_____

What embarrasses you about your anger?

_____

_____

_____

What is it about your anger that your spouse, family, and friends object to most?

_____

_____

_____

Name three ways in which you have attempted dealing with life's problems by not directly addressing your anger.

_____

_____

_____

Names three ways in which you have delayed a real commitment to your recovery.

_____

_____

_____

UNMANAGEABILITY

What does "unmanageability" mean to you?

_____

_____

_____

How has your life become unmanageable in the following areas due to your anger?

Do you see yourself as being under control? Explain

_____

_____

_____

Have you been able to control your family" Explain

_____

_____

_____

Have you been able to control your jobs or bosses? Explain

_____

_____

_____

Have you been able to control your health? Explain

_____

_____

_____

Have you been able to control your spiritual life? Explain

_____

_____

_____

How much control have you had over your sexual life? Explain

_____

_____

_____

What goals have you set for your life?

_____

_____

_____

Do you feel that these goals are achievable if you continue to misuse your need to control?

_____

_____

_____

List three feelings, which you have reacted to when you started to control some person, place, or thing.

_____

_____

_____

People, Places & Things

*We admitted that we were powerless over people, places, & things
—that our lives had become unmanageable.*

Give some examples of how you have tried to control other people.
List three separate instances.

_____

_____

_____

Give three examples of how you have manipulated people in order to
control being in a particular place.

_____

_____

_____

Give some examples of how powerlessness (loss of control) has revealed
itself in your experience while trying to control someone.

_____

_____

_____

List some times when you started out "in control" but then "lost control."

_____

_____

_____

Can you recall any episodes when you were not trying to control something and those around you were? What did this feel like?

_____

_____

_____

Has there been any physical abuse to yourself or to others as a result of you trying to control other people, places, or things.

_____

_____

_____

If you continue to try to control people, places, & things what do you think will happen?

_____

_____

_____

How has the misuse of your power endangered your life or the lives of others? List three separate instances.

_____

_____

_____

What embarrasses you about the misuse of your power?

_____

_____

_____

What is it about your behavior that your spouse, family, and friends object to most?

_____

_____

_____

Name three ways in which you have attempted dealing with life's problems by not directly address your misuse of power?

_____

_____

_____

Names three ways in which you have delayed a real commitment to your recovery.

_____

_____

_____

UNMANAGEABILITY

What does "unmanageability" mean to you?

_____

_____

_____

How has your life become unmanageable in the following areas due to your attempt to control?

Do you see yourself as being in control? Explain

_____

_____

_____

Have you been able to control your family" Explain

_____

_____

_____

Have you been able to control your jobs or bosses? Explain

_____

_____

_____

Have you been able to control your health? Explain

_____

_____

_____

Have you been able to control your spiritual life? Explain

_____

_____

_____

How much control have you had over your sexual life? Explain

_____

_____

_____

What goals have you set for your life?

_____

_____

_____

Do you feel that these goals are achievable if you continue to misuse your need to control?

_____

_____

_____

List three feelings, which you have reacted to when you started to control some person, place, or thing.

_____

_____

_____

Gambling

We admitted that we were powerless over gambling—that our lives had become unmanageable.

How has gambling endangered your life or the lives of others? List three separate instances.

_____

_____

_____

Names three behaviors that you are ashamed of as a result of your gambling.

_____

_____

_____

What is it about your gambling that your spouse, family, and friends object to most?

_____

_____

_____

Give some examples of how you have tried to control your gambling.

_____

_____

_____

Give some examples of how you have lost control of your behavior as a result of gambling.

_____

_____

_____

List some times when you started out "in control" but then "lost control" by gambling more than you intended and suffered the consequences.

_____

_____

_____

Can you recall any episodes when you were not gambling and those around you were? What did this feel like?

_____

_____

_____

Has there been any physical abuse to yourself or to others as a result of your gambling?

_____

_____

_____

Why would you want to stop gambling? If so, give three reasons.

_____

_____

_____

Name three things you have blamed for your problems instead of your gambling.

_____

_____

_____

Name three ways in which you have attempted dealing with life's problems by not directly addressing your gambling problem.

_____

_____

_____

Name three ways in which you have delayed a real commitment to your gambling problem.

_____

_____

_____

UNMANAGEABILITY

What does "unmanageability' mean to you?

_____

_____

_____

How has your life become unmanageable in the following areas?

How do you see yourself?

_____

_____

_____

How have you managed your relationship with your family?

_____

_____

_____

How have you managed your relationship with your friends?

_____

_____

_____

How have you managed keeping jobs for long periods of time?

_____

_____

_____

How have you managed your physical health?

_____

_____

_____

How have you managed your spiritual life?

_____

_____

_____

How have you managed your sexual life?

_____

_____

_____

If you continue to gamble, what do you think will happen?

_____

_____

_____

What goals have you set for you life?

_____

_____

_____

Do you feel that these goals are achievable if you continue to gamble?

_____

_____

_____

List three feelings that you have tried to alter through your gambling.

_____

_____

_____

Food

We admitted that we were powerless over food—that our lives had become unmanageable.

There was a very good reason that the founders of the AA program placed the emphasis on powerlessness over alcohol. Many times we have observed people taking powerlessness for granted or with a casual attitude. Understanding powerlessness must be the foundation for any successful approach to the recovery from eating disorders.

POWERLESSNESS

How has your use of food endangered your life? List three separate instances.

_____

_____

_____

Names three behaviors that you are ashamed of as a result of your eating habits.

_____

_____

_____

What is it about your eating behavior that your spouse, family, and friends object to most?

_____

_____

_____

Give some examples of how you have tried to control your eating or purging.

_____

_____

_____

Give some examples of how you have lost control of your behavior as a result of food.

_____

_____

_____

List some times when you started out "in control" but then "lost control" of you're eating and suffered the consequences.

_____

_____

_____

Can you recall any episodes when you were following your eating plan and those around you were eating everything in sight? What did that feel like?

_____

_____

_____

Has there been any physical abuse to yourself or to others as a result of your of food problem?

_____

_____

_____

Do you want to get your eating under control? If so, give three reasons.

_____

_____

_____

Name three things you have blamed for your problems instead of your eating disorder.

_____

_____

_____

Name three ways in which you have attempted dealing with life's problems by not directly addressing your eating disorder.

_____

_____

_____

Name three ways in which you have delayed a real commitment to your eating disorder.

UNMANAGEABILITY

What does "unmanageability" mean to you?

_____

_____

_____

How has your life become unmanageable in the following areas?

How do you see yourself?

_____

_____

_____

How have you managed your relationship with your family?

_____

_____

_____

How have you managed your relationship with your friends?

_____

_____

_____

How have you managed keeping jobs for long periods of time?

_____

_____

_____

How have you managed your physical health?

_____

_____

_____

How have you managed your spiritual life?

_____

_____

_____

How have you managed your sexual life?

_____

_____

_____

If you continue overeat or purge, what do you think will happen?

_____

_____

_____

What goals have you set for you life?

_____

_____

_____

Do you feel that these goals are achievable if you continue to overeat or purge?

_____

_____

_____

List three feelings that you have tried to alter through the use of overeating or purging.

_____

_____

_____

Made in the USA
San Bernardino, CA
10 March 2017